Colour and Create
Vintage War posters

*20 Poster designs to help
release your creative side*

Connect with us online to
- Share your colourings with other colouring enthusiasts
- Get free downloads of some of our designs
- Find out about our up-and-coming books
- Get discounts and enter competitions

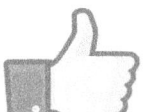

Our Facebook Page:
www.colourandcreate.com/facebook

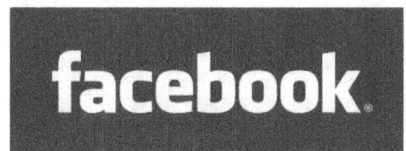

Our Facebook group:
www.colourandcreate.com/facebookgroup

On Twitter:
www.colourandcreate.com/twitter

On Pinterest:
www.colourandcreate.com/pinterest

Colour Test Page

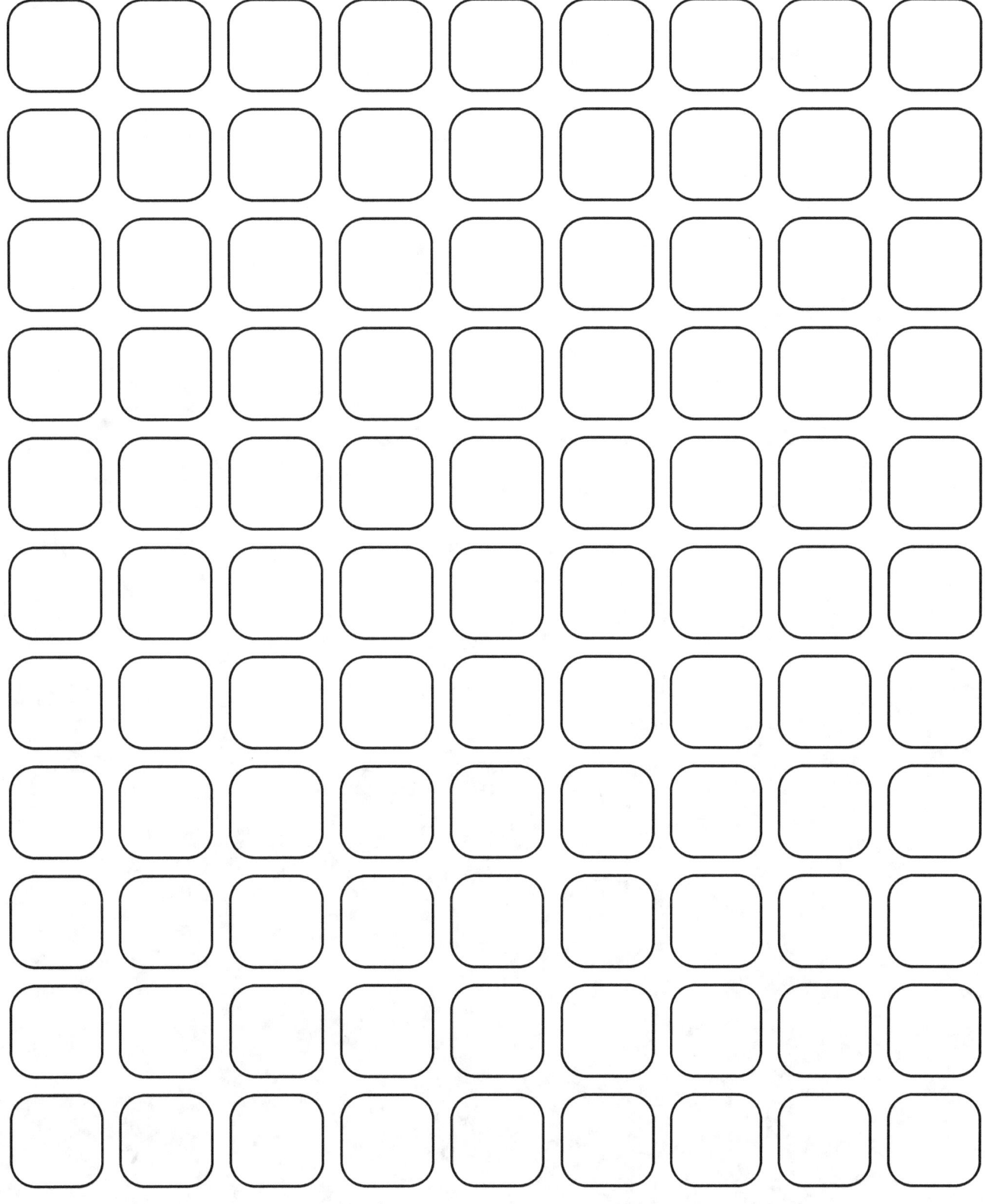

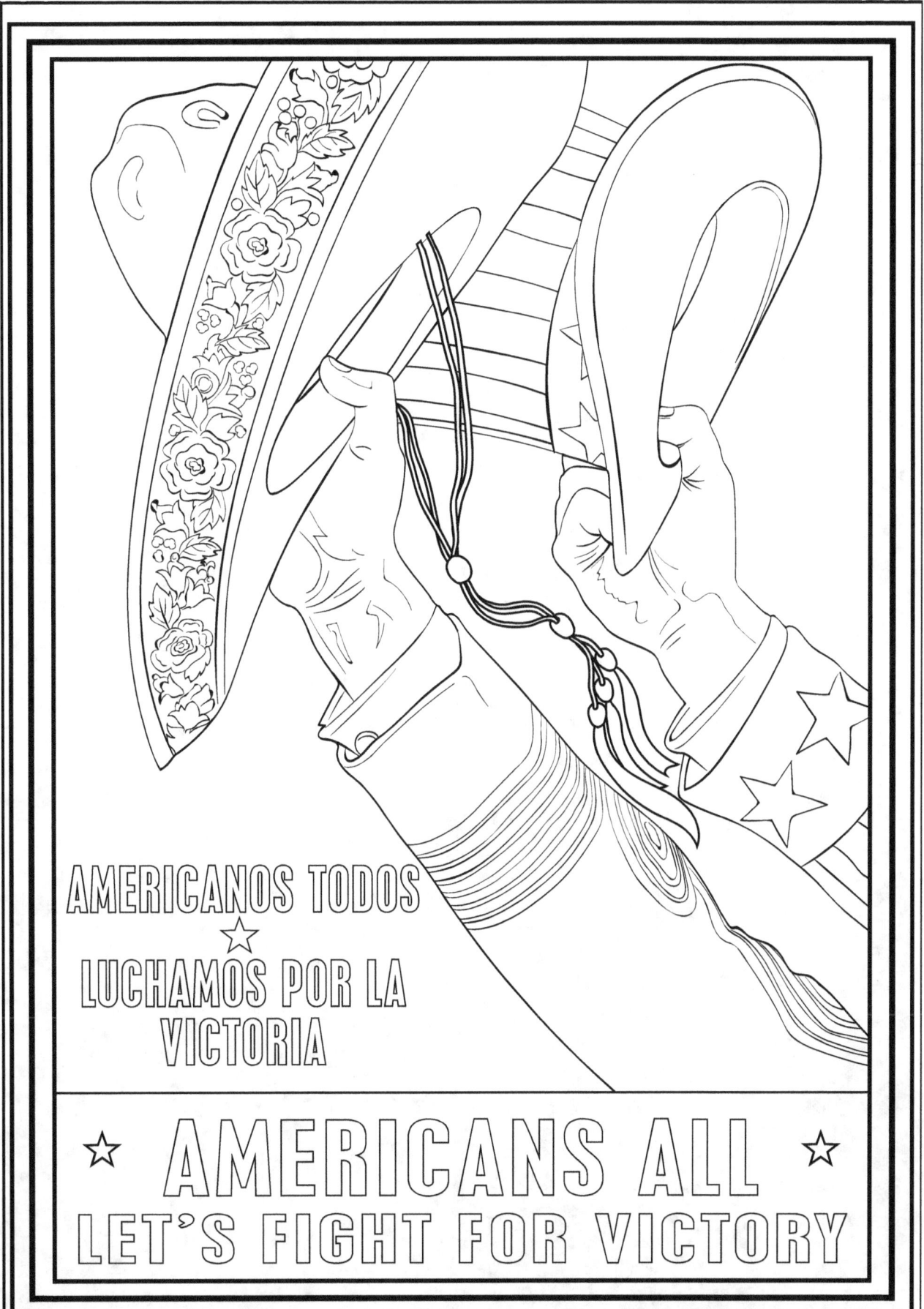

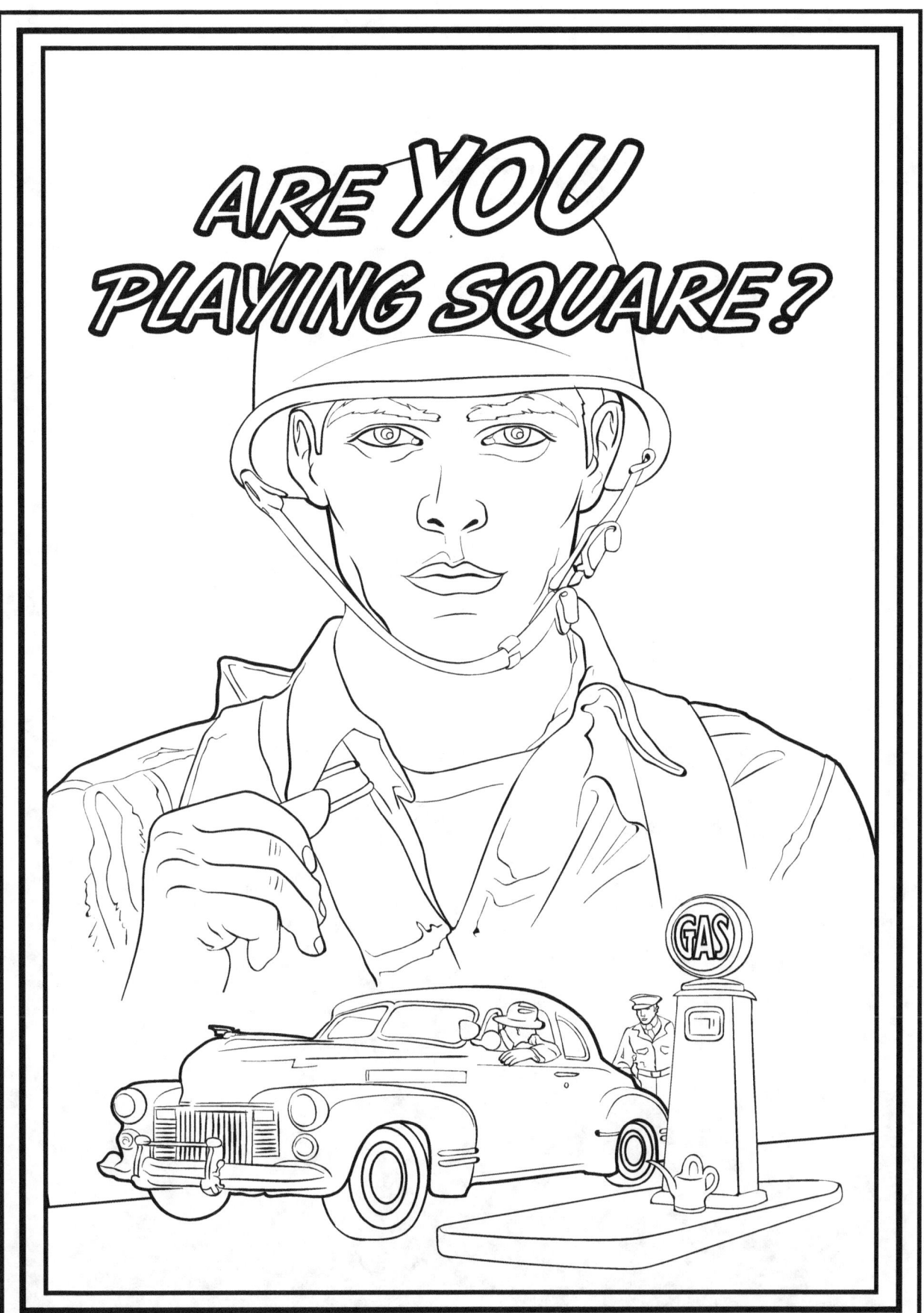

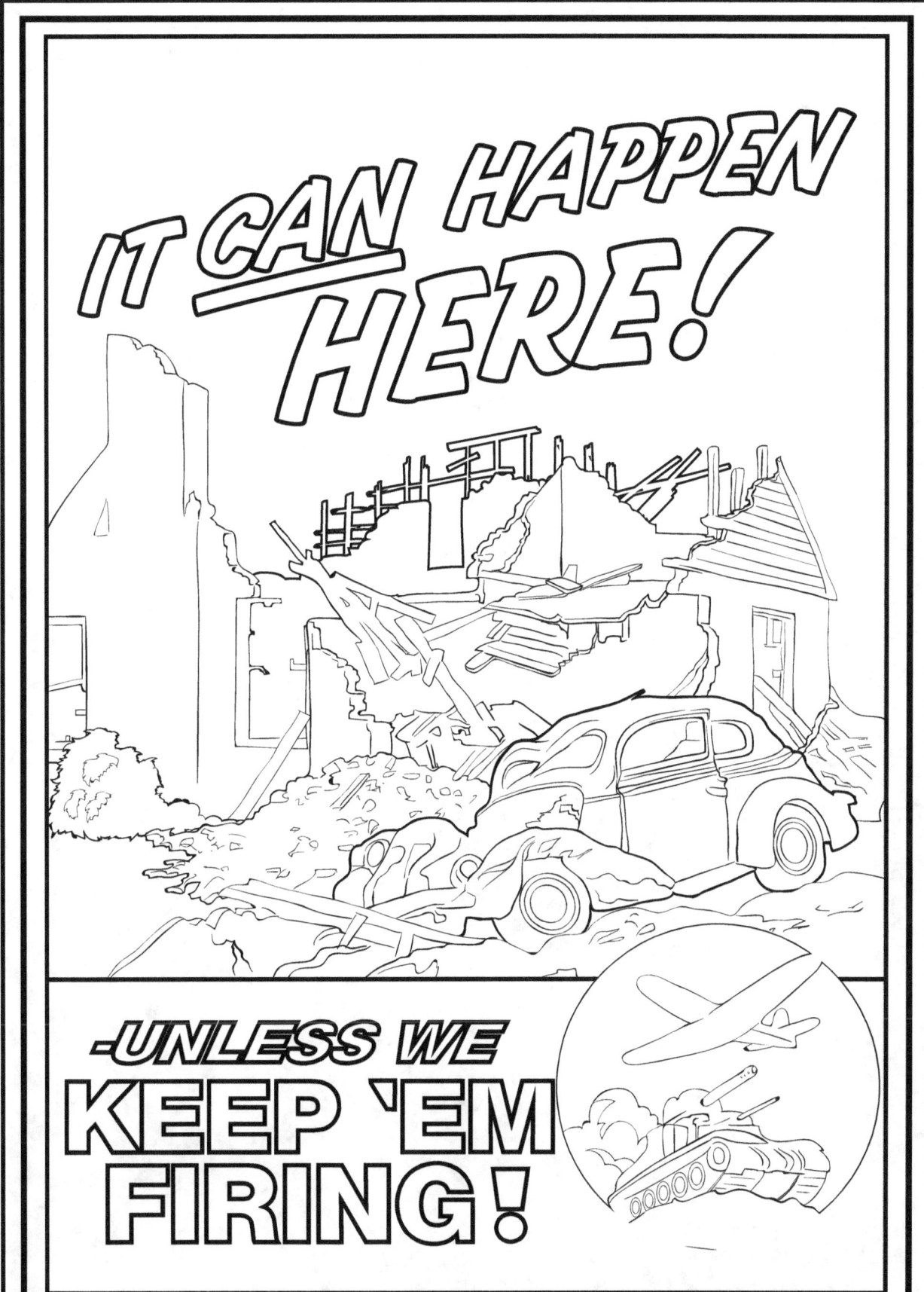

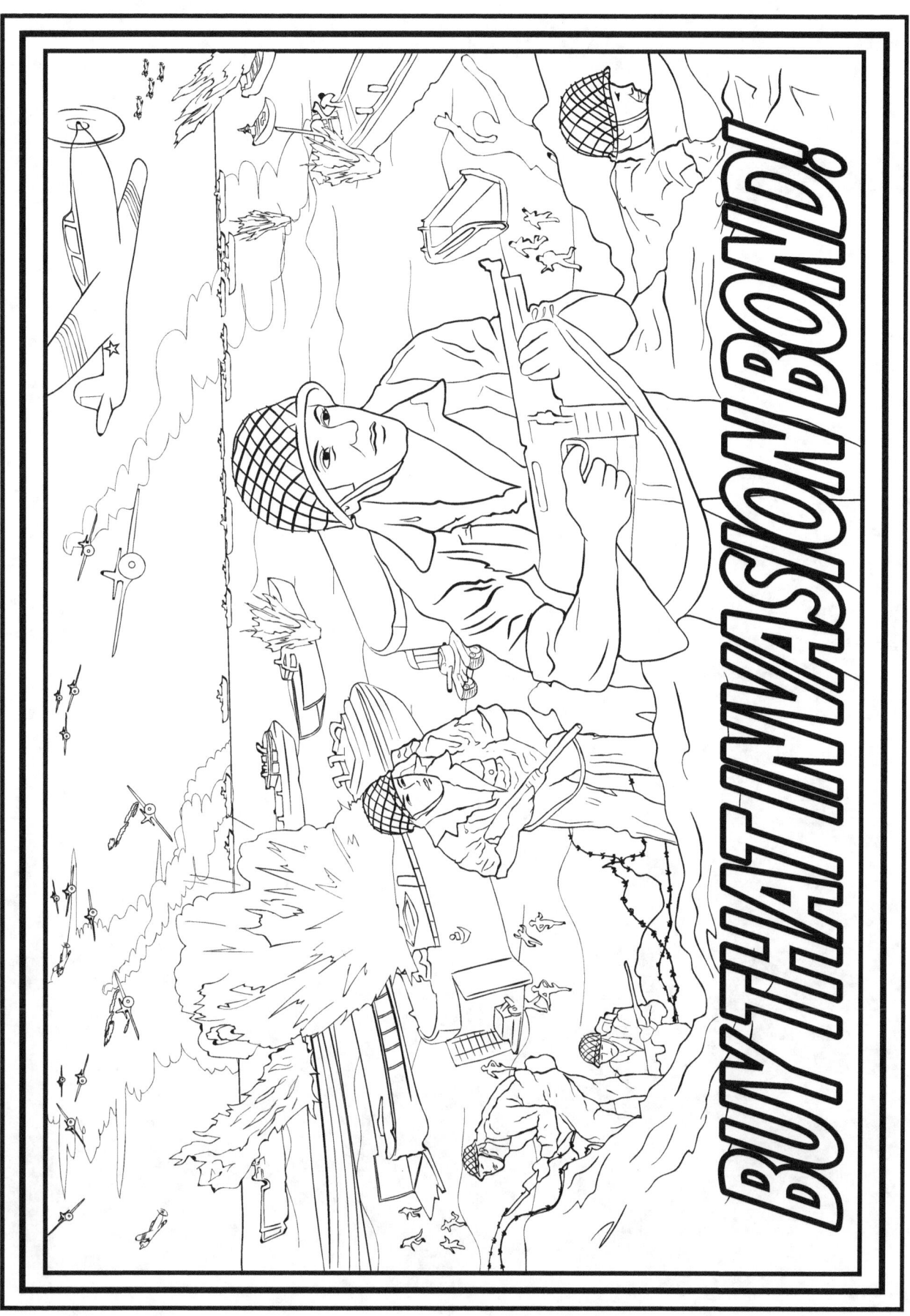

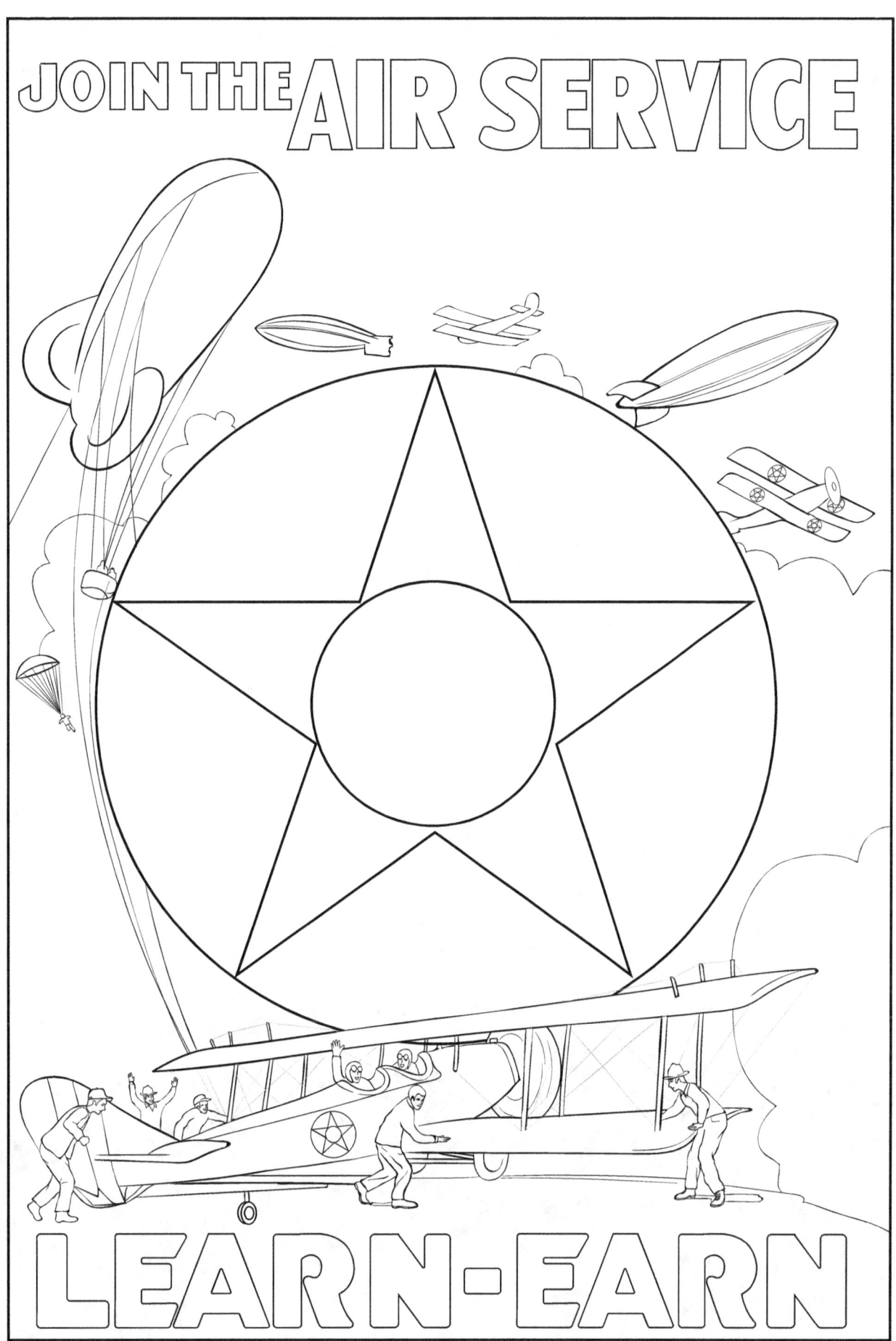

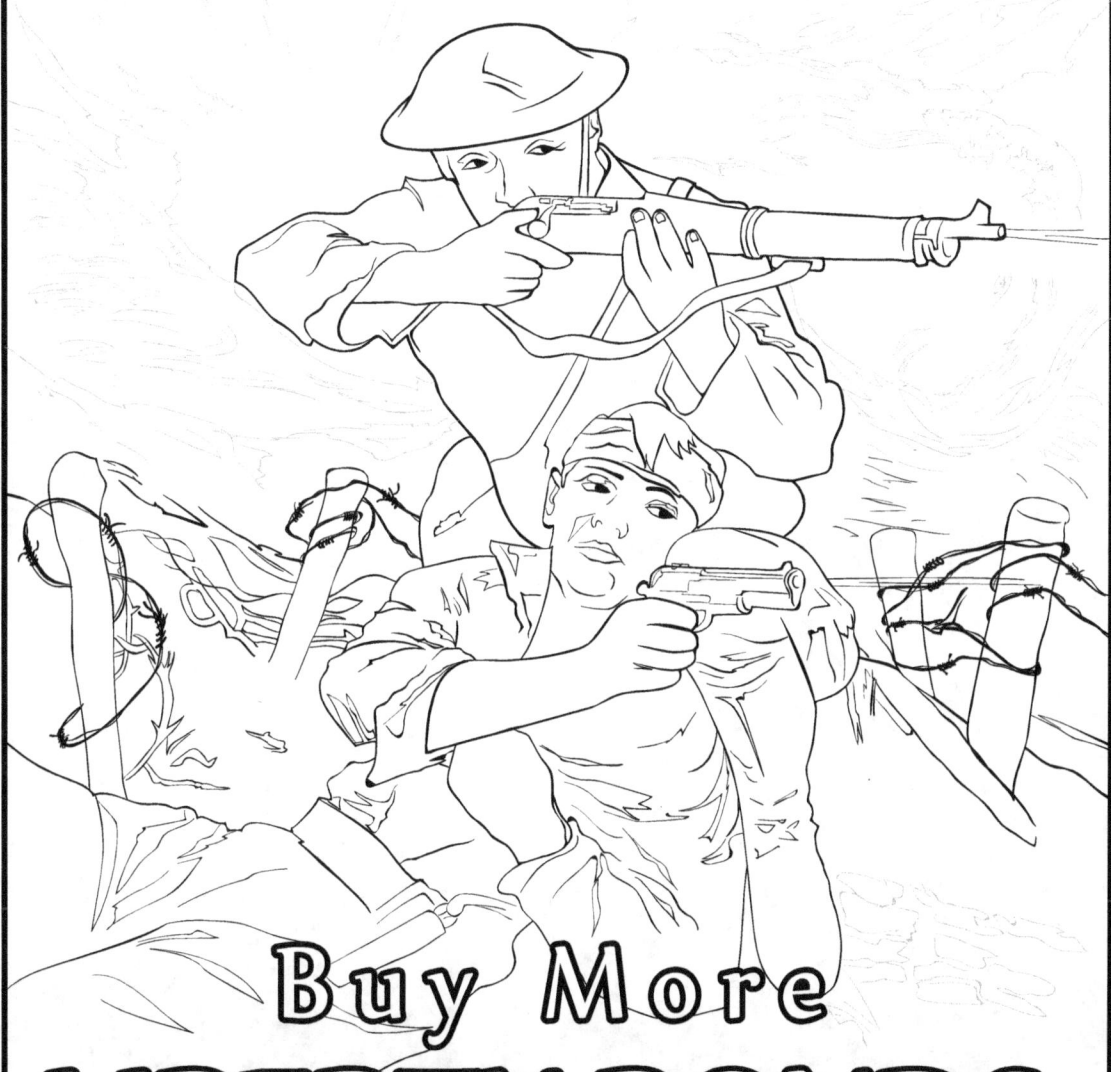

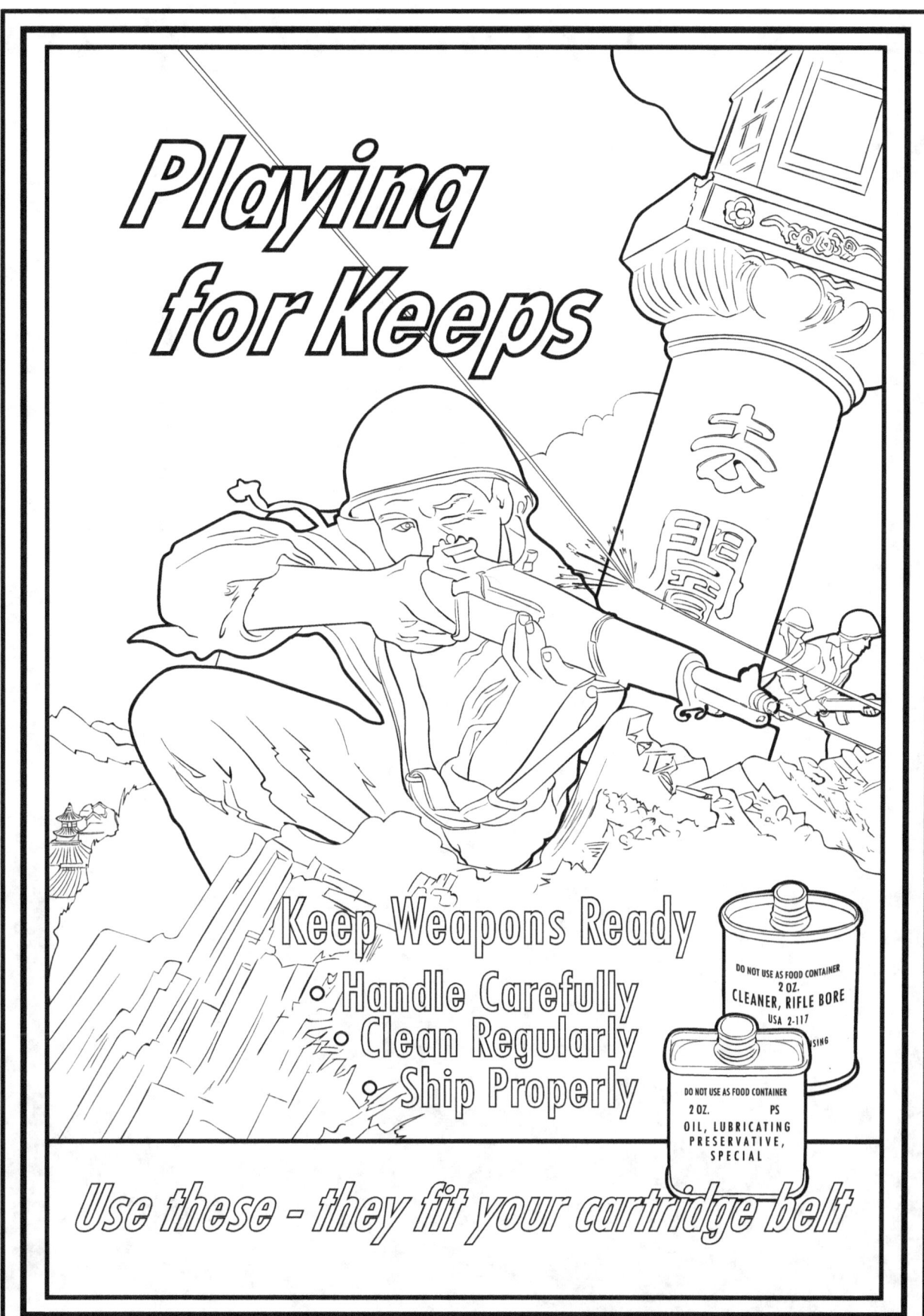

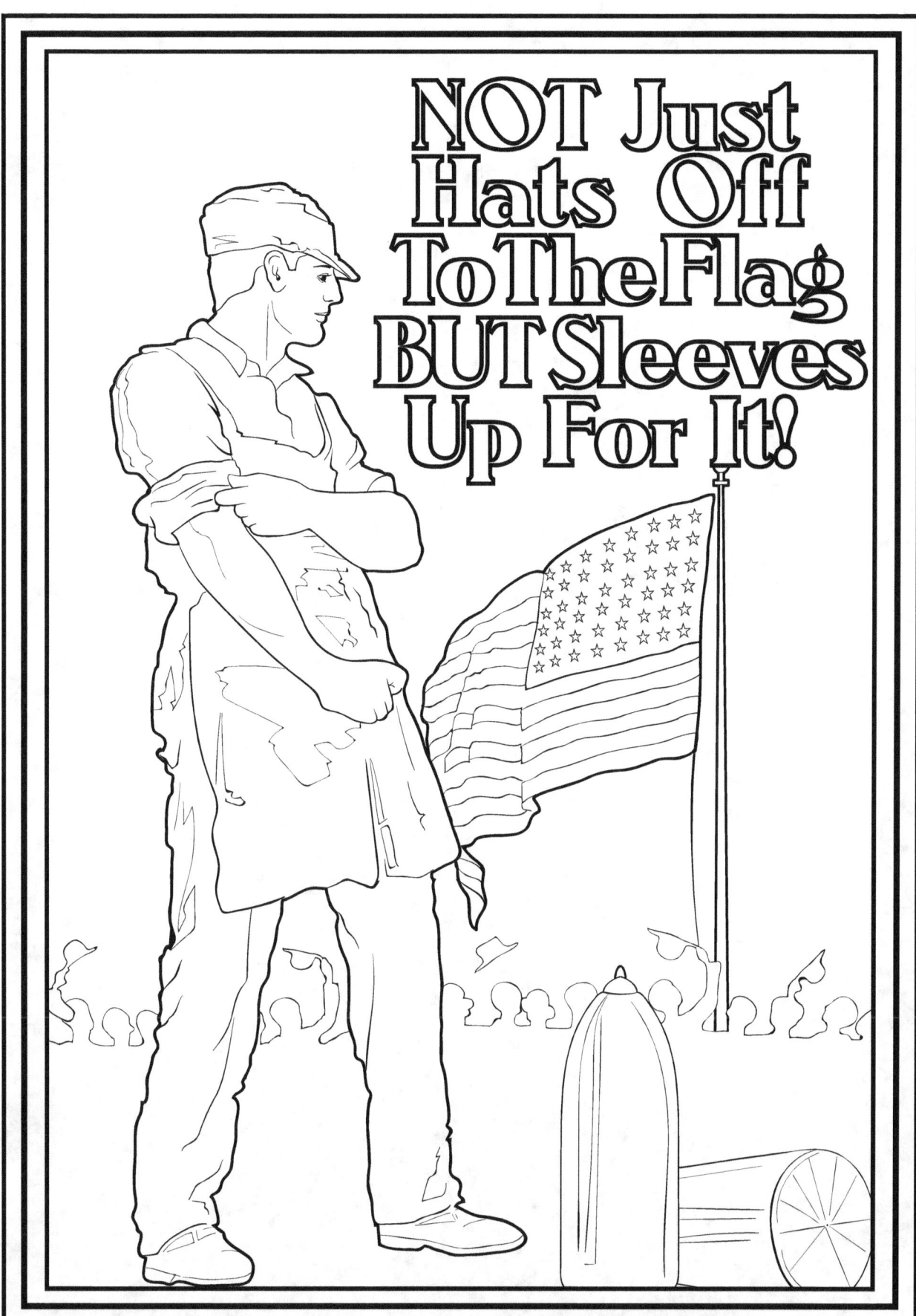

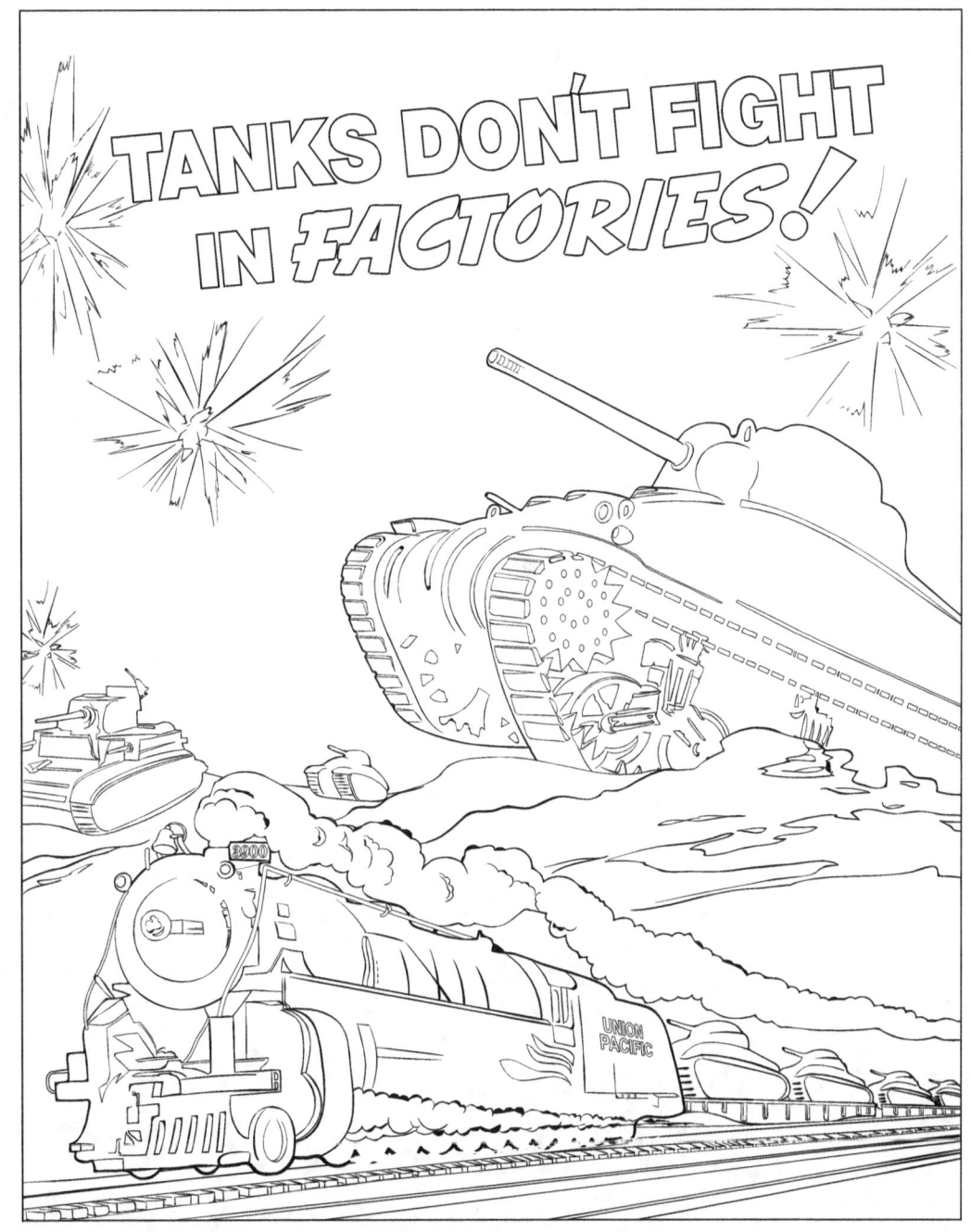

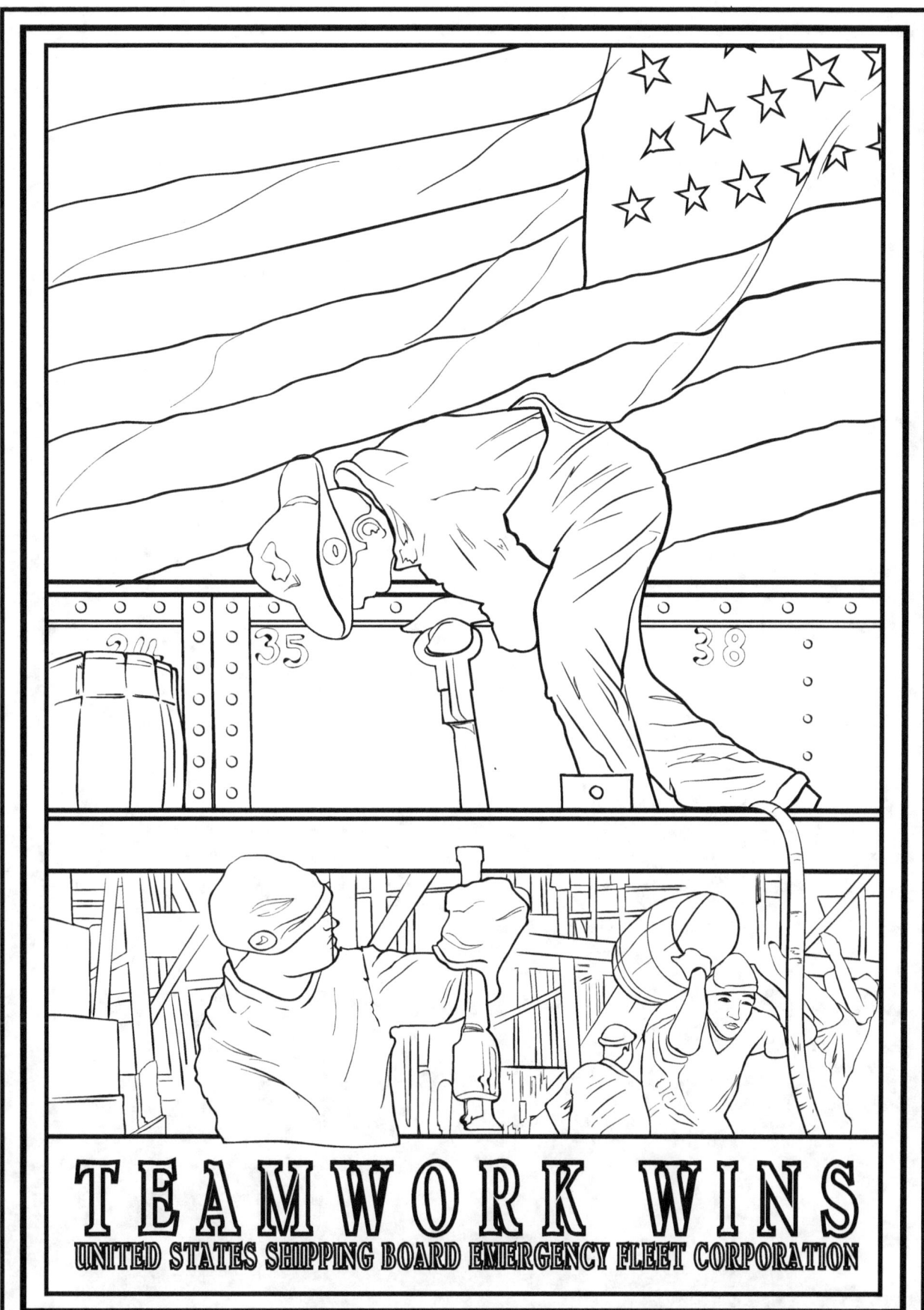

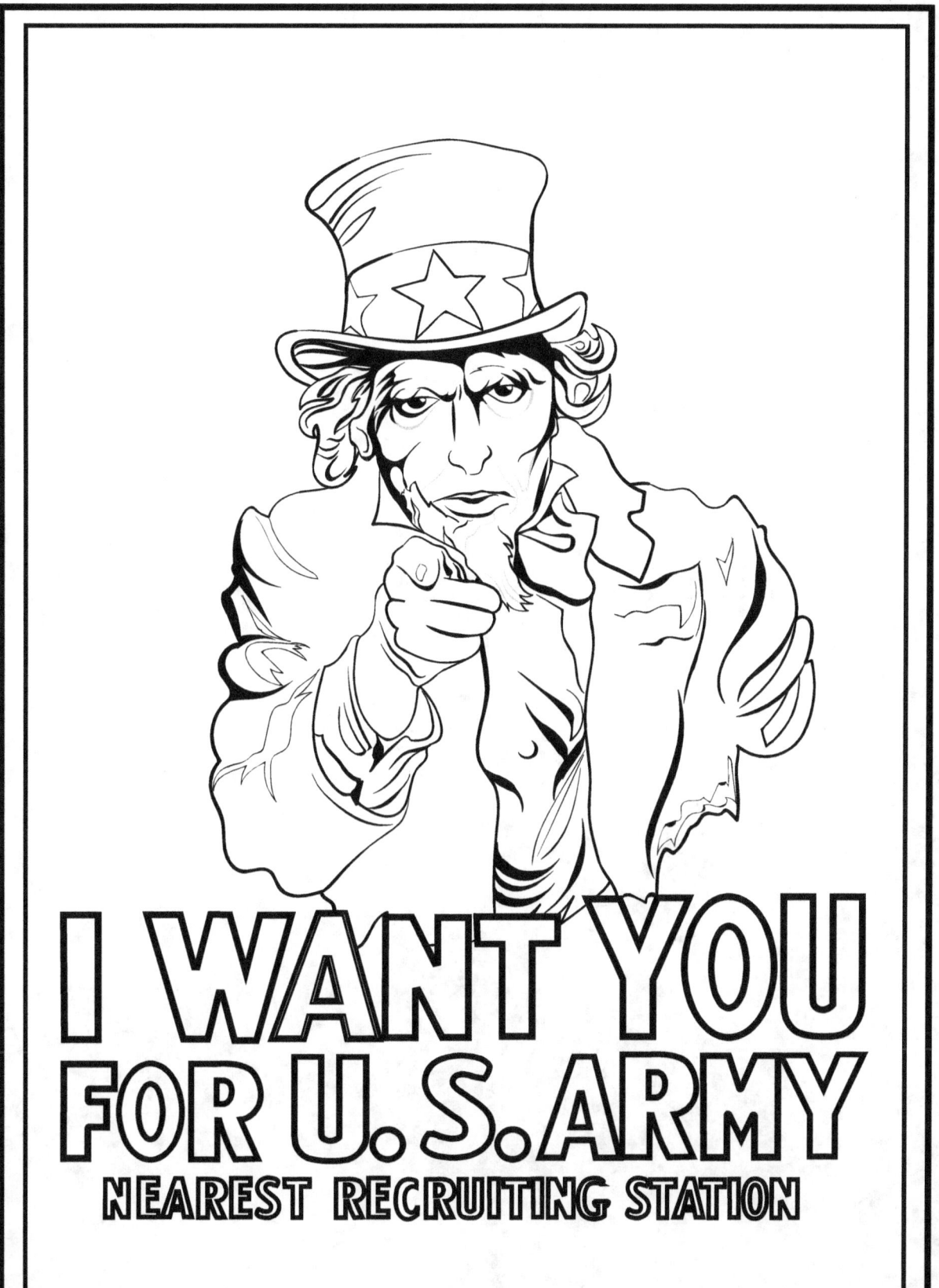

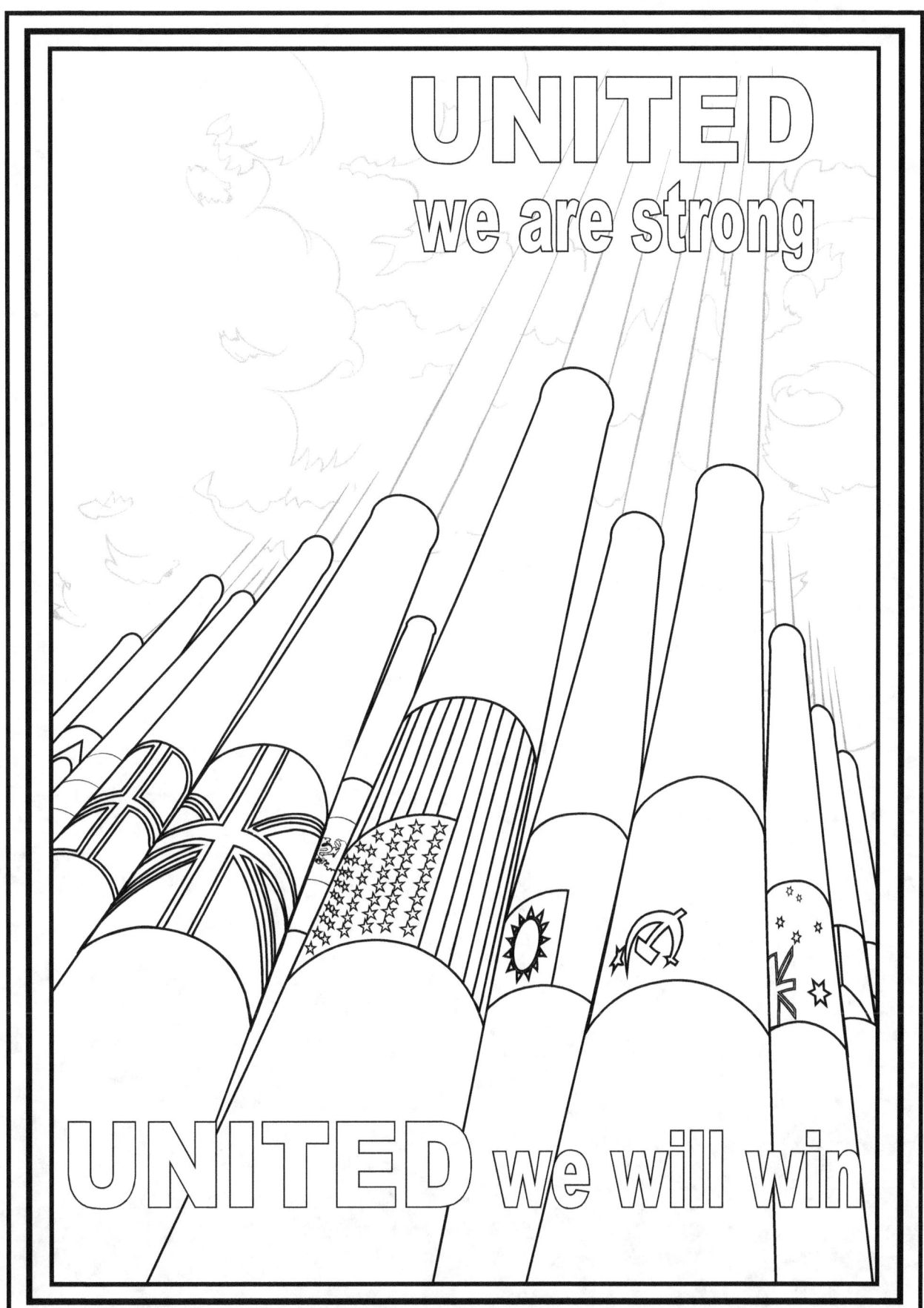

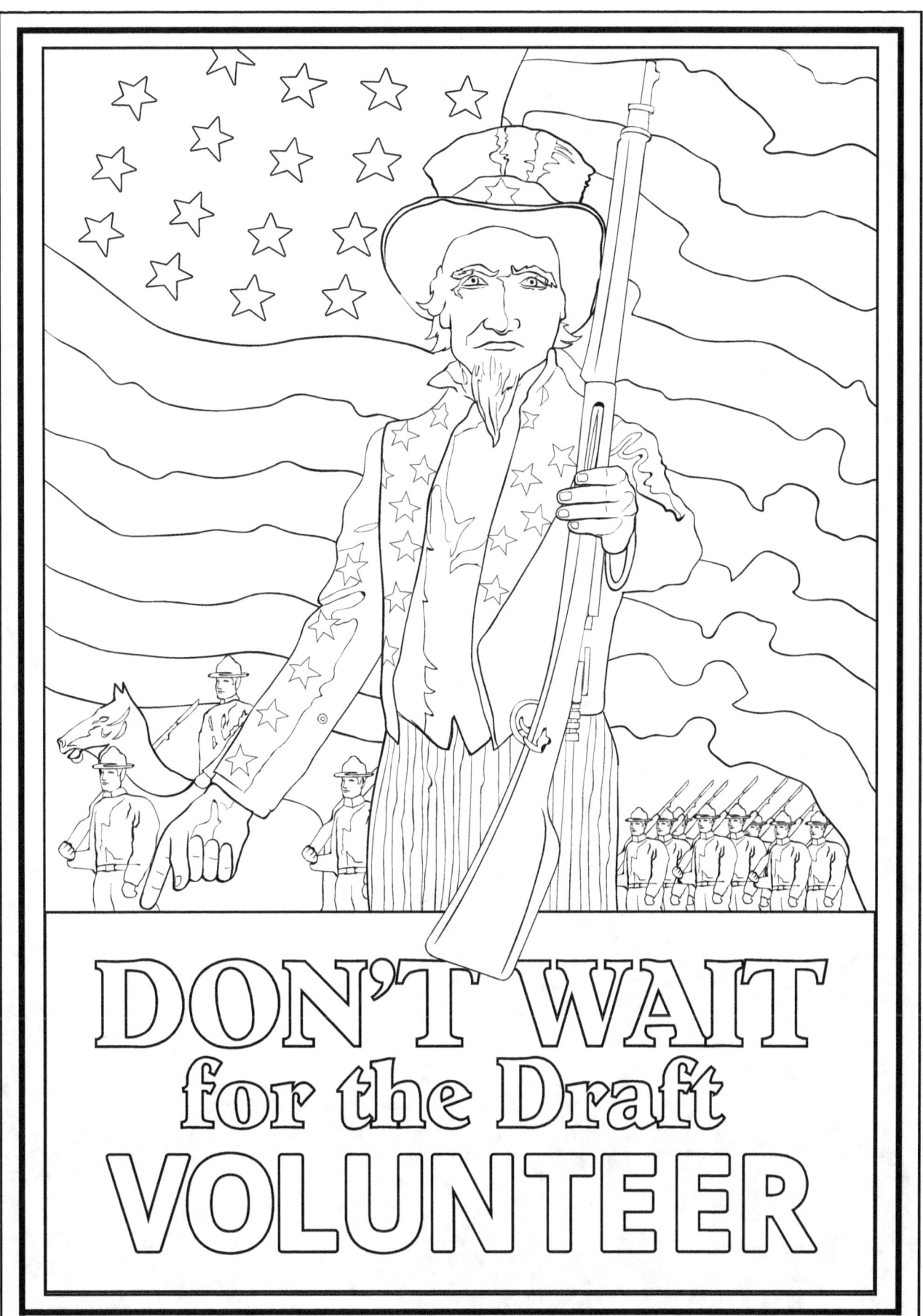

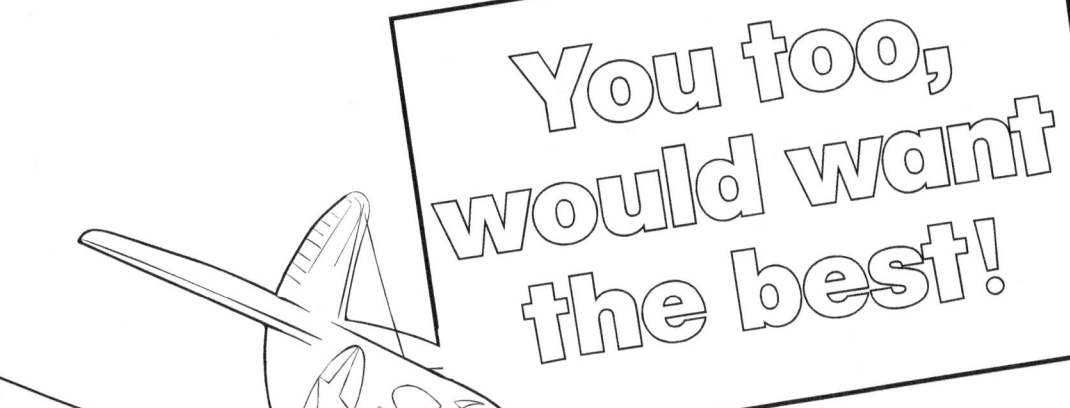

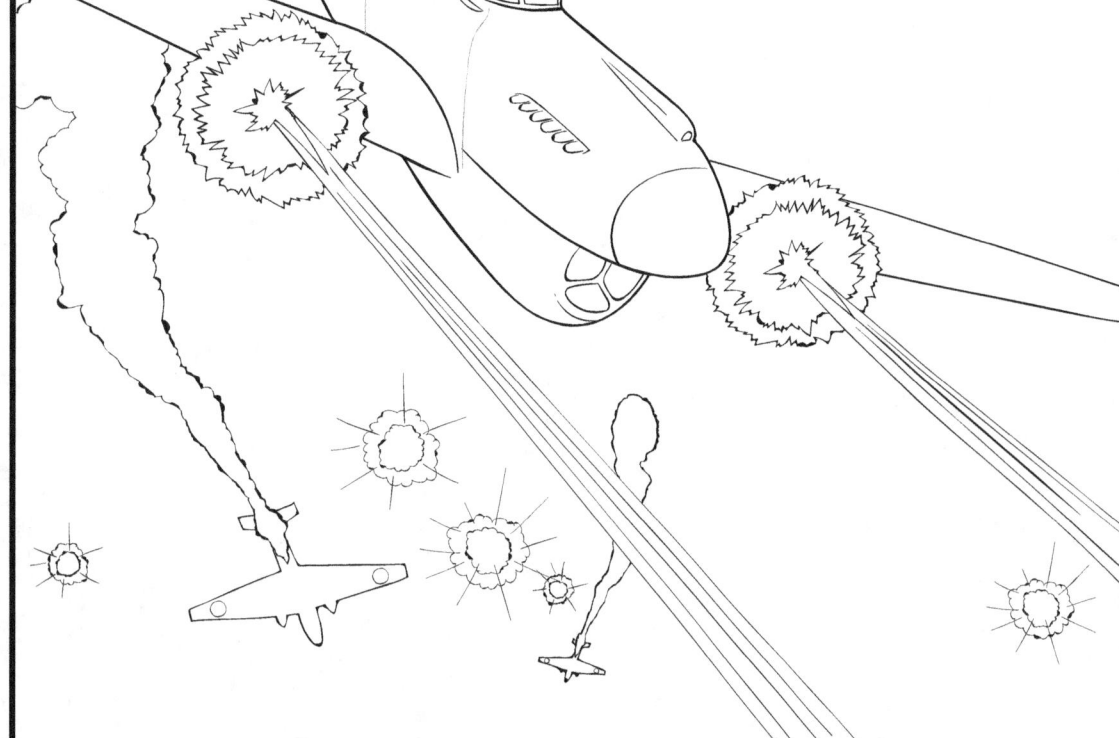

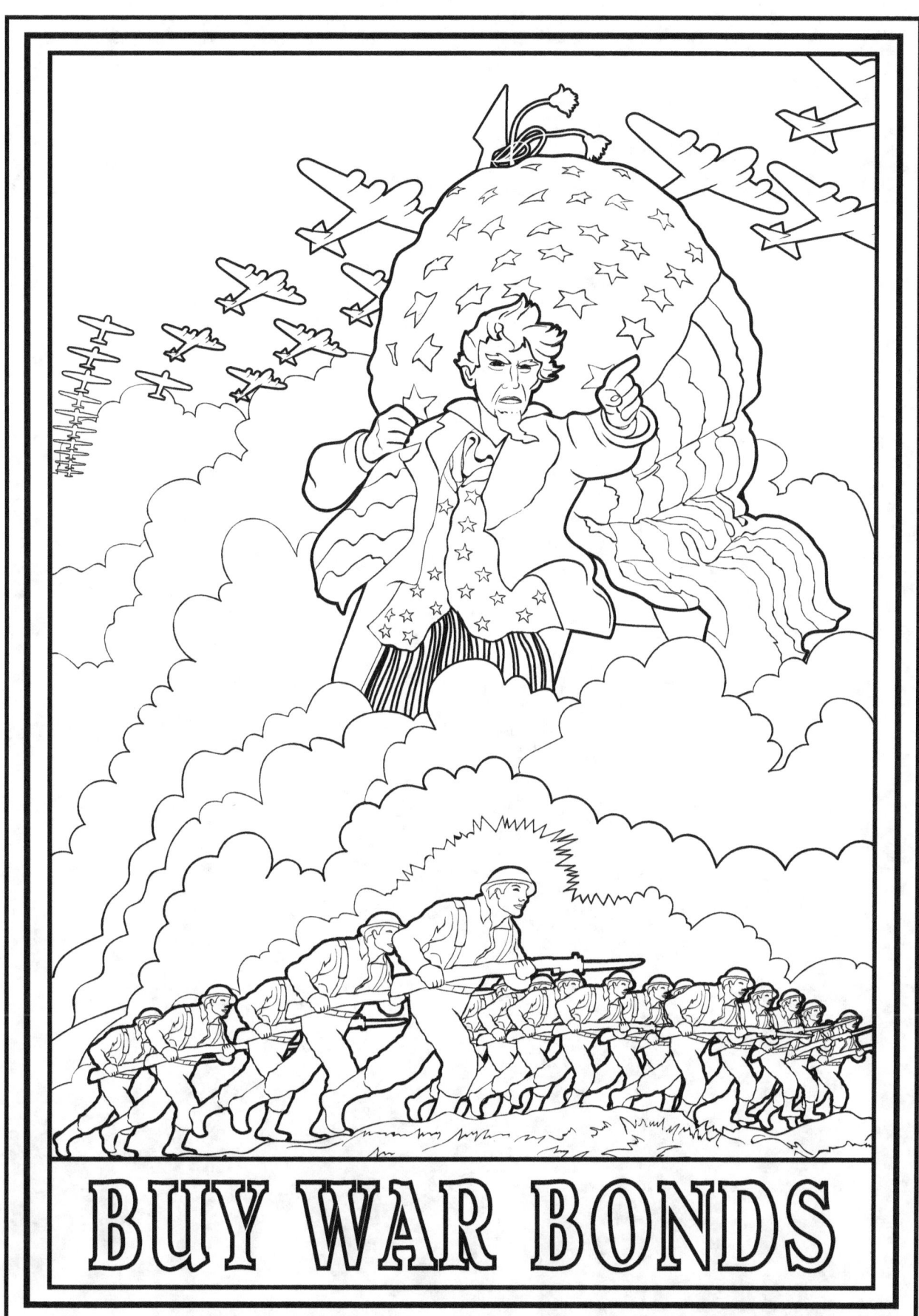

BUY WAR BONDS

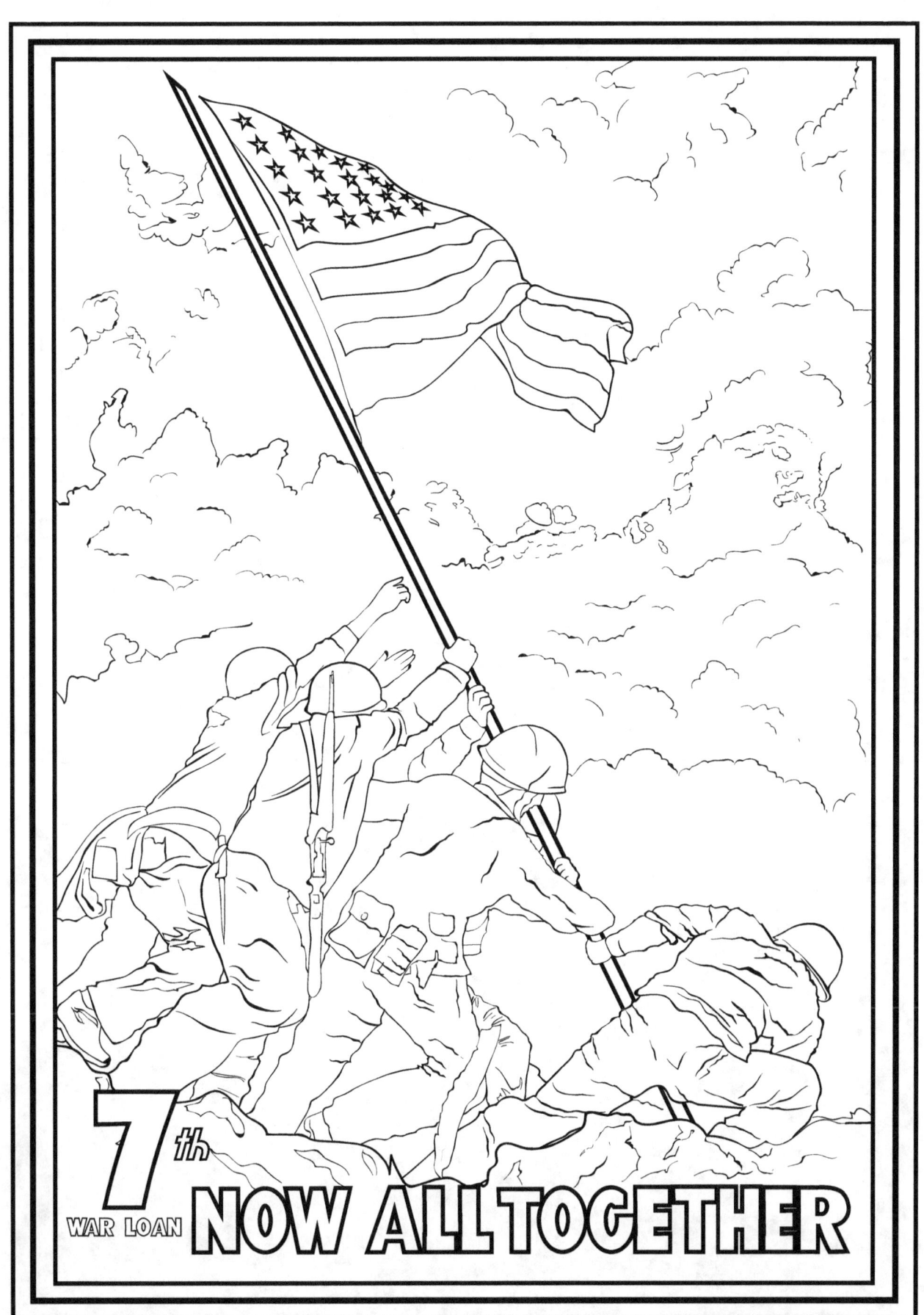

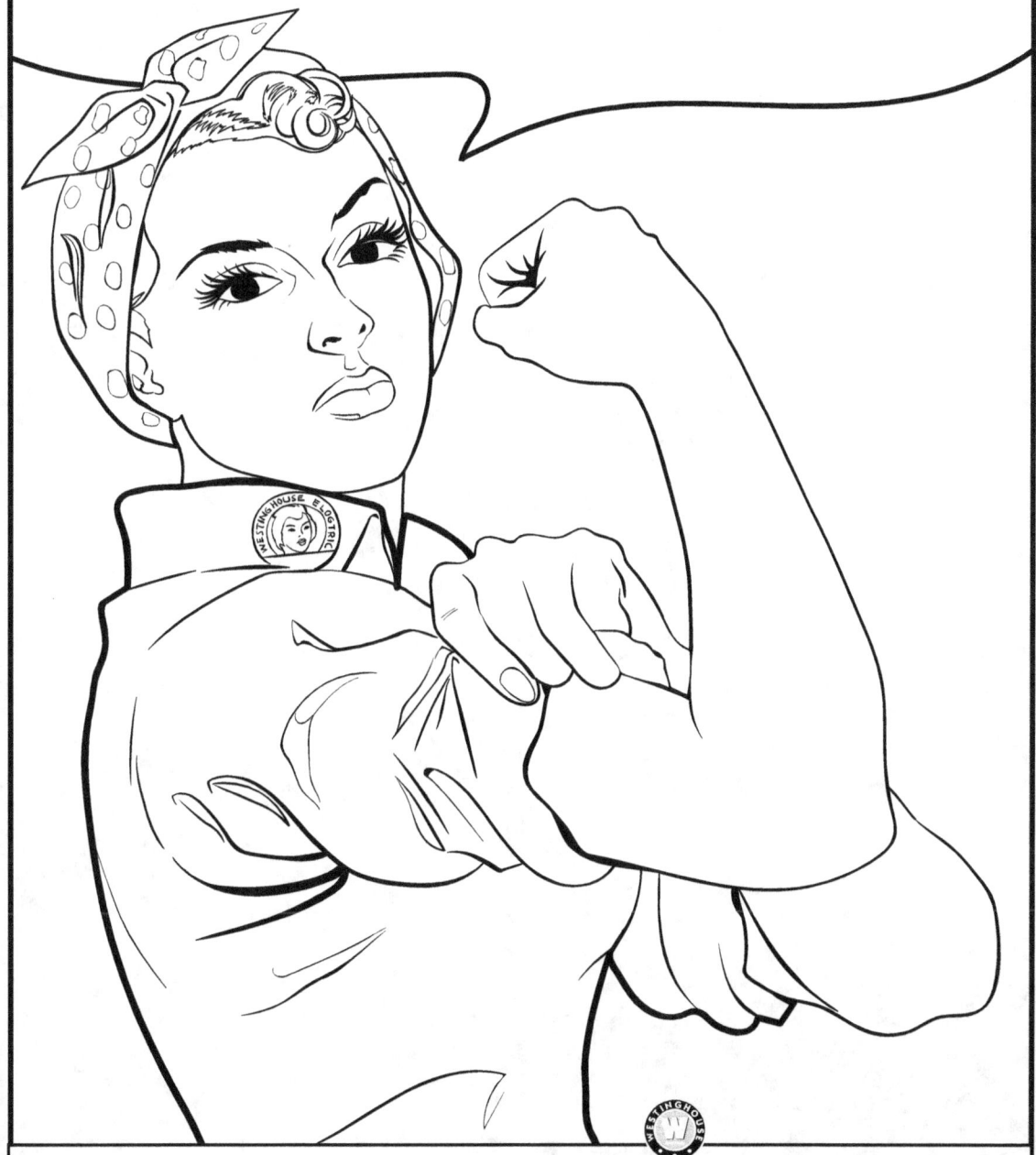

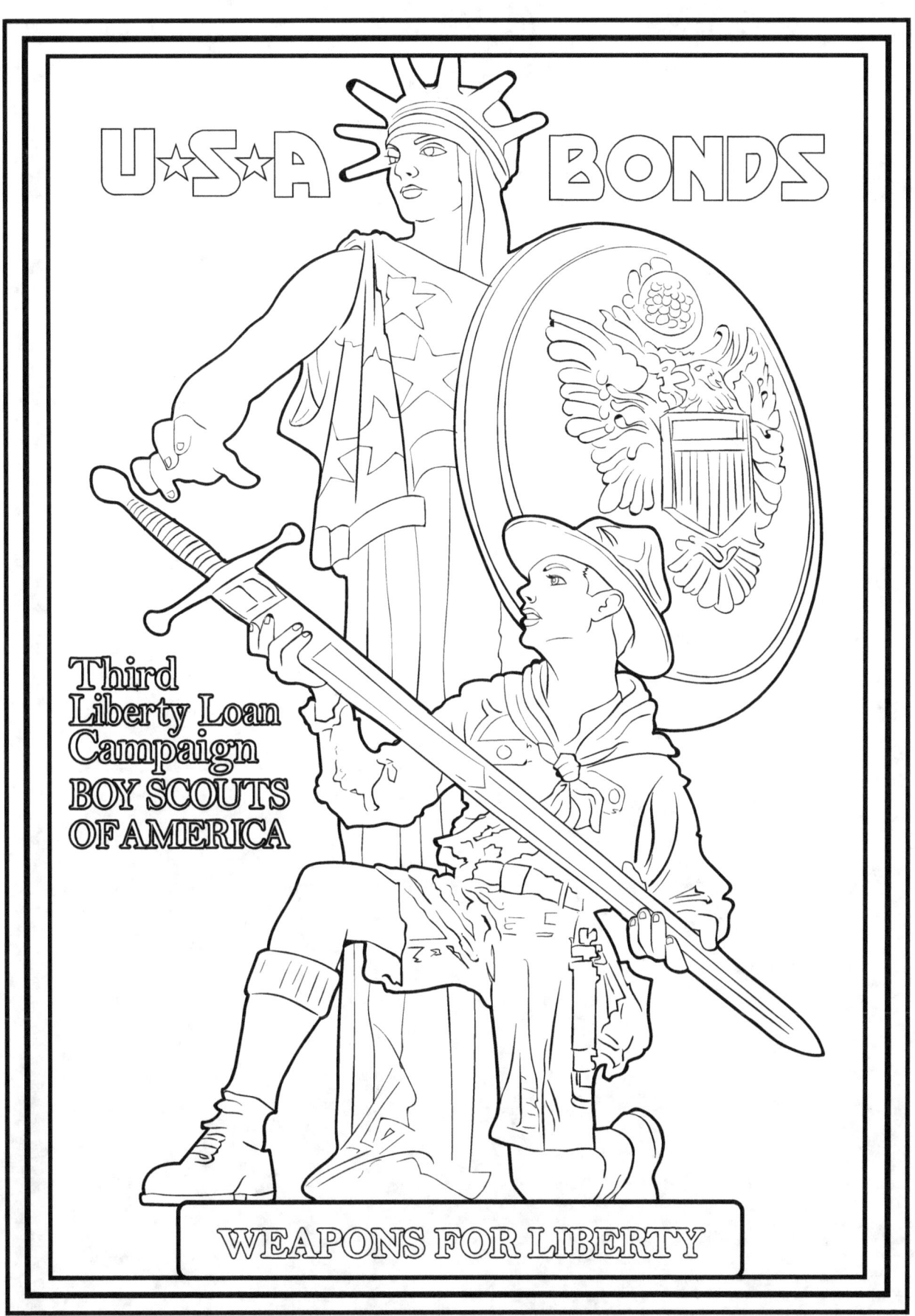

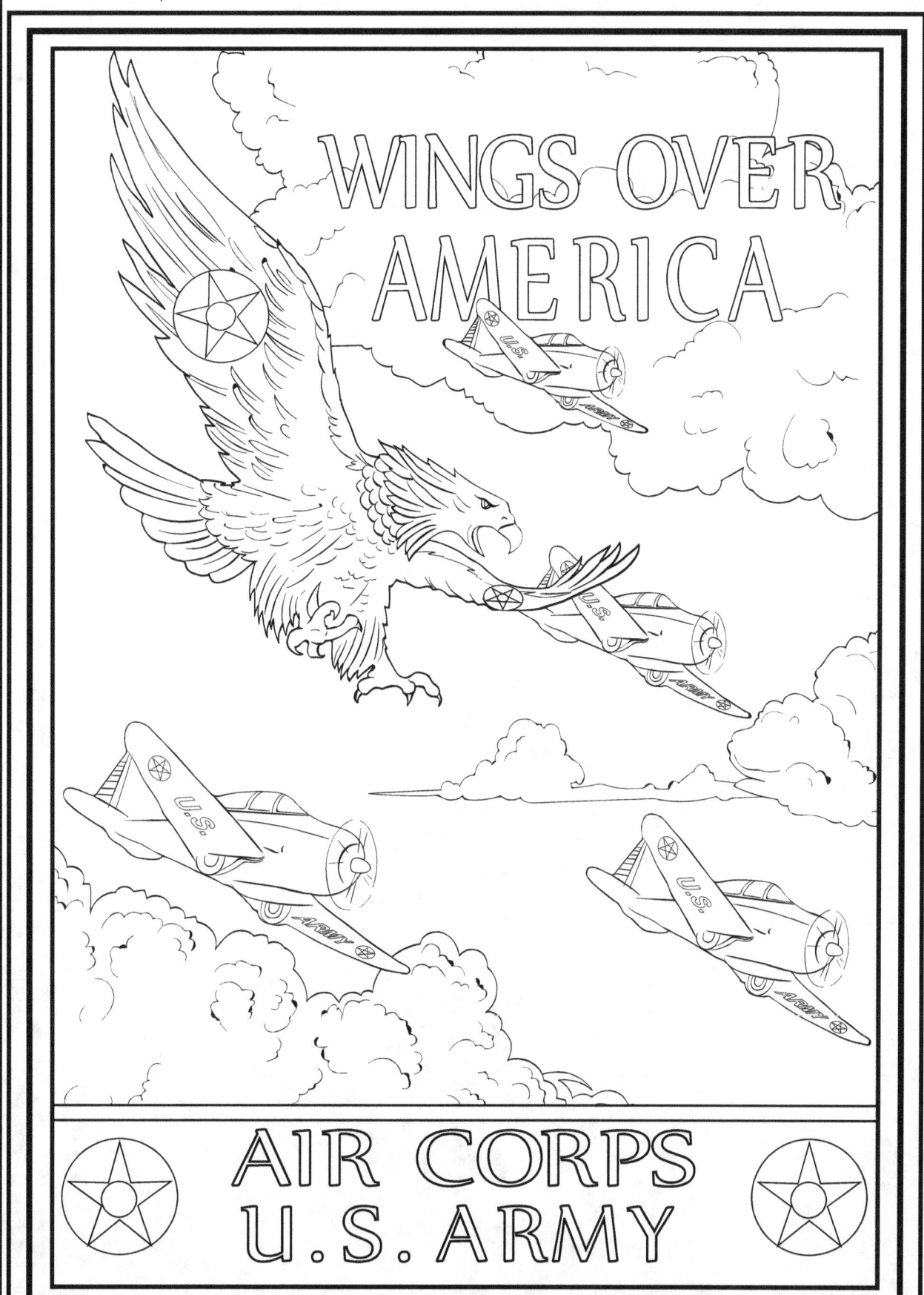

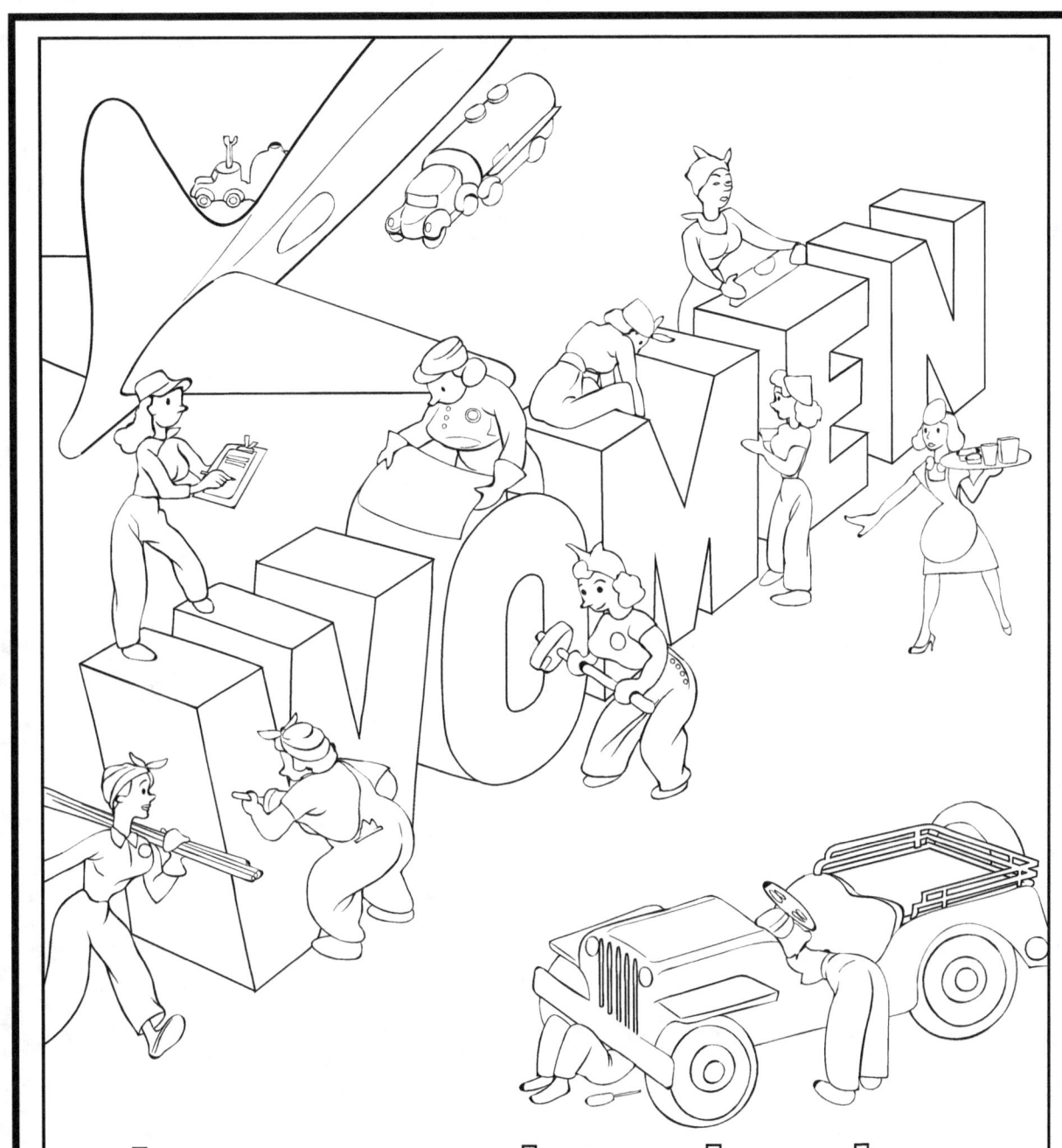